Om Sri Ganesha

Dedicating this to my two little dinosaurs, my lovely sons!!!

Acknowledgement

Thanking all the great books out there that helped feed my knowledge and research. Thanks to google, all my mentors, friends and family members that inspired me, impacted me to write this book.

Table of Contents

Preface

How are you? Are you happy? Do you go to bed at night every day with a smile and heart filled with happiness? Whatever is your answer, if you are anyone who is working hard day in day out and riding a rollercoaster of Happy and Unhappy feelings, or if you are surrounded by people who tells you that there is no lasting Happiness, this book is a must read.

This book if for those who desire happiness in life, especially long lasting happiness for real. This book delivers a deep dive into creating a happiness medium around you which will work with you and for you to generate a wealth of abundance that is everlasting. This book is for those who have or are suffering from unhappiness or stress in life because of work, work-life, kids, parents, in-laws, relationship, money, passion, health, social media, comparison or any other factors. Create your Happy Frame is about 'YOU', it is a driver to navigate you through the finding of your unique value, your unique thoughts and your unique perceptions to generate a truly happy you and creating an ability to sustain the happy frame for rest of your life.

You probably picked up this book wondering what is "Create a Happy Frame"? and how can one create a happy frame and how does it work? Create Your Happy Frame is a concept that establishes extreme clarity on how you perceive happiness and success. It provides you with a toolset of actions you can take to create success and happiness.

Introduction

Not sure why scary things always happen at nights, it was late in the night when my uncle and aunt started fighting and he hit her and she was crying and yelling and cursing words and more hitting and yelling it went on for a longest hour or so in my life. I was terrified and trembling with fear and cried for help. Back in the day there were no cell phones to call my parents to come get me and more importantly to help my aunt who was getting beaten up, I thought she was getting killed. Never witnessed this kind of violence in real time. This was supposed to be a fun sleepover with my aunt and cousins and it turned into a never forgetting terrifying experience for me, I was a 6 year old at that time and that was my first taste of grown ups, married life which made a lifetime impact on me and till date I get worried in the nights that something bad is happening somewhere.

I am a very passionate individual with a strong drive to help women and families cope up with relationship in life, especially single parents and married parents, because I love kids, I love happy families and I cannot imagine any kid to go through pain and concerns for safety and insecurity. What drives my passion is my experiences and the spark inside me that had kept me wondering what I can do to make things better in this world. After several years of witnessing rough relationships and realization of some fundamental basics of relationship, I am writing this book with an honest intent to help families and couples out there in relationship to self-solve for the day to day struggles and to help build happy life by applying some of the principles and simple basics of relationship.

This book will provide a step by step walkthrough to dealing with problems and disputes in relationship at every stage of a relationship, the primary focus being on newly in relationship, relationship after kids, relationship with both spouses working and single parents. Human beings are social animals and we spend (with social media we used to rather) most of our life in/around some relationships, parents, friends, spouse, partner's, kids, co-workers etc and our happiness is often influenced by these relationships to an extent. There is a phase in everyone's life when we look for our life partners (at least that is the intent), all goes well we might find one and then what happens to our happiness?

I have grown up in a culture of arranged marriages and have witnessed some rough relationships. Wife and husband struggling through their relationship and how things get worse in most cases with arrival of kids in a relationship. I have witnessed and experienced how kid's feelings and emotions are impacted when parents are less in love and more in fights and arguments. It is a feeling of insecurity, a feeling of fear, feeling that there is no true love, feeling of aggression, low-confidence, a strong feeling in the heart as if the heart is melting and pain in the brain. My heart fills with tears every time I witness anyone going through relationship problems and especially when I see kids watching parents fight or parents yelling or punishing kids because they are frustrated with their spouse and vent out on innocent kids. Due to the many struggles and fights I have seen families go through since my childhood, I had a strong opinion for marriage and relationship and believed that marriage and relationship comes with lots of struggle, pain and sorrow.

Some interesting observations from my real-life experiences and experiences of my close friends and family. <u>Couples fight really bad and then they make up for it</u>. As a kid, I would get scared and terrified when two people fight. I observed that there is a recurring pattern where one of the partners is always compromising and tolerating the fights to go on with the marriage or just to stay together for the sake of kids. I grew up watching the same pattern over and over again.

My friends, cousins, my sisters got married, then in few months or years same pattern of fights: start fighting for many reasons, domestic violence, broken nose when a husband hit his wife during a fight, injuries when an aggressive husband attacks wife in a heated dispute and pushes her against the wall. I noticed in some cultures, couples just fight in front of their kids not to mention shamelessly in front of relatives too, seeing those young kids cry while parents quarrel is heart-breaking. I was still young, but my blood would boil up to take some action against the violence and the arguments itself. But never had the courage to go against the culture and the norms. I grew up watching and hearing more stories about painful marriages and relationships going through rough times. My heart used to go for the kids and the families every single time and every single time I would come back to the same question, how can I prevent this epidemic. Why cannot people have a decent relationship with healthy conflicts and no violence?

Is it really a fairy tale about living happily ever after?

I would think and think about it and as usual would do nothing about it and I am pretty sure there are many out there who can understand exactly what it means to go against it. Meanwhile, I had to focus on my studies and meet my parent's expectations to become a great professional. Which I became one eventually. However, I still had a strong corner for all those women and men going through relationship problems and all the kids in the families with unstable relations. Deep down I wanted to do something someday and this is one of many ways I would like to contribute to the community. I did a lot of research and I wanted to get to the root cause of why there is no lasting happiness in a relationship, what is the root cause of some of the fights? what can be done to prevent it. I studied the psychology of human thinking and what triggers in one's brain that makes people say and do things that tears apart the happiness medium which is created with lots of love and care.

This book is a forum to enlighten the couples and families and young men and women who are going to get married or going to get into a relationship one day. Life, Marriage and relationship need not be painful if one or both in the marriage has a broader mindset and create their happy frame, to live happily! In the next few sections I will take you deep into some of these concepts to understand that root cause.

Marriage

According to WIKI:
Marriage/matrimony/wedding is a union of two individuals legally making their relationship public and making vows to common responsibilities, beliefs and values.

Another definition:
It is a legal bonding of a woman(wife) and a man (husband) to enter a new chapter of life.

The way I see it, there are two primary kinds of marriages in the world, one where parents/family/friends chooses your partner and get you married (also known as arranged marriage), the other where you choose your own partner (love marriage or love arranged marriage).

Arranged Marriage

In an arranged marriage, parents search for a "rightly qualified" future daughter/son in law and once a suitable match is found they meet up the girl and the boy. If parents on both sides like the girl/boy and most of the times, the boy/girl should also like each other, without knowing each other (wonder how that happens, it does though). Arranged marriage is driven by parents and the girl and boy will get engaged to eventually get married. There is a lot of unknowns in an arranged marriage, the girl and boy should get to know each other and their families after the marriage. Since the spouse is chosen by the family members often they have similar cultural beliefs and values, that will be expected to follow by the girl usually and embrace the same values.

Love Marriage

Love marriages are resulted out from loving their partner before marriage. A boy and a girl like each other, usually date for sometime, they fall in love during the process and eventually may get married. Also, while dating there are breakups very often, when the boy and girl realize they are not in love or they are not made for each other etc. In a more matured communities and western cultures, dating more than one person to assess if they will become good partners after marriage is very common and in this process finding the right person to marry takes place. Although love marriage has many flavors, the basic point is that the boy and girl know and like each other way more than in a typical arranged marriage.

So one can quickly think and conclude, love marriages are the ideal way to go with marriage, since love marriages are based on knowing each other, and you love the person you are marrying, in a love marriage. Isn't life going to beautiful if everyone goes with a Love marriage then, right? Wrong, not really, research shows that about 40 to 50 percent love marriages result in a breakup/divorce. And divorce rate in an arranged marriage is about 4.4 percent. Pretty- promising divorce rate in an arranged marriage for not knowing your spouse prior to marriage, right?

Does it mean couples are unhappy in an love marriage and breaking up or does it mean couples are happy in an arranged marriage and are staying together? none of these guesses are right. I have done a lot of research in this matter and many case studies and observed many couples. What keeps a couple together from divorce or break up in many cases is fear, fear of change, fear of losing the kids, fear of losing respect, fear of insecurity, fear of society, fear of not able to find someone again, fear of facing the reality etc. Also, in many cases, true love keeps them together, love for the kids, love for the happy moments spent prior to losing the magic, love for the parents etc.

Before we get into details of what is happening in a relationship and why couples get onto a rough stage in every marriage, let's look at what is happening in a relationship prior to marriage.

Before marriage, there is a phase in life when you are in love or dating someone special or your wedding is arranged and you are with your fiancé, there is a different chemistry at this stage between the two. Either they are learning about each other, or trying to impress each other, try to look their best, be more funny, spend more money, gifts exchange, first kiss, holding hands, looking forward to meet next day, long phone calls all night and meeting early mornings. Every one of us have gone through this phase at one or the other time in our relationship. If you remember properly, that flying butterflies inside the tummy, fast heartbeats, sweating when it is super cold, special feeling of touch when you hold your partner are some of the feelings. All of these feelings are positive and energizing which makes you look forward for the next meeting with your partner. Supporting each other, taking things easy, trying to be ok with mistakes made, expressing feelings. This is typically how pre-marriage time travels for the most part. There will be occasional quarrels, or missing each other, not talking to each other etc. but, they all are recovered with a sorry, date nights, making up for them with gifts and hugs and kisses etc. At a big picture view this phase is mostly memorable with happy moments. It makes the couple think that they are in true love, and that rest of their life will be similar to the experience they are going through, and that they should marry each other and live happily ever after.

If that is the case, then once they get into a bond of marriage because they love each other so much, why are they not happily married ever after. What is happening after Marriage?

Let's take a look at the psychology behind marriage!!!!

Majority of the couples are entering a relationship because they "Love" each other or at least they think they do or their parents think they will make a good wife/husband. From the couple's perspective, love is sometimes, "I love your body", "I love making love to you", "I love that we have common interests", "I love the money your parents have", "I love the money you are bringing with the marriage", "My parents like you, I don't care if I Love you or not" etc... I think you understand what I am trying to point out here. Many times what a couple is thinking love is not just love instead it is love with an expectation, they are after some expectation out of this relationship. And the point many of us are not preview to or are educated on, is that marriage/relationship comes with responsibilities. How many of us knew how to manage finances to pay monthly bills, save money, spend wisely before marriage and let alone raising kids? Chances are most of us did not. Even if we had knowledge, we are very in-experienced.

Couples enter into this relationship thinking of a bright future ahead. Women especially in arranged marriage look forward to a great time with her husband, luxury gifts, social status, and hoping all of her dreams to come true in the form of her spouse (her ideal prince charming).

Men enter a marriage/relationship expecting respect in the community and in the family, love/love making with the wife, a wife to take care of his family and house and himself, places to visit with the wife, the fact that he can be a man to his wife.

These are just a few expectations from men and women entering into marriage or relationship, there are many more to list.

The focus here is, it stands out very clearly, the expectations are different from a wife and a husband's point of view. These different expectations and new discoveries every day about each other and the family members play a vital role in how a marriage/relationship is going to travel through the journey of life.

Why Relationship?

Before we form a strong opinion about marriage and relationship, I do want you to know that being in a relationship is a wonderful experience and it has more positive impacts if one can learn to enjoy their relationship.

There are many advantages of being in a relationship or married, that outweigh all the struggles and problems that we face with relationship. Marriage or relationship is a beautiful episode of life that everyone should enjoy and those who excel at it should take great pride of success. Quick bits on benefits of marriage:

- ❖ You have someone that appreciates you and your personality the way it is
- ❖ You have a partner to share your happy and sad times that you are facing in your life
- ❖ You have someone that knows you well enough to give love and care to you and bring a smile on your face when you need the most

- You can have a family and kids together
- You can make love to the one you love over and over
- You have someone that can take care of you and your kids
- You have someone to help financially (couples can leverage each other's income)
- You can enjoy vacations and travel as a family
- You have someone that can cover your back when you are in trouble
- You have someone to understand and encourage you to become successful
- You gain a motivation to provide better living to your family
- You get a sense of completeness by marrying, that now you can focus on accomplishing your purpose in life
- When you come home late after working hard all day, there is someone at home waiting to see you and is grateful for all the hard work
- You are more complete than you are by yourself

- ❖ You have someone to grow old with and spend your retired life
- ❖ You can raise emotionally strong kids as a couple
- ❖ Not to forget the most important <u>You Are Not Alone</u>

The list goes on, these are only a few benefits listed, there are many resources out there on the internet if you want to search for, which will cover many more benefit areas of being married including, financial, mental, physical areas. The point I want to make with the benefits of being married is that, in this fast-paced world, where life can get super complicated and super frustrating, there are many success and failures a person will face more than ever and the amount of stress everyone is going through to make their mark in this world is increasing tremendously, it is so required to have that human interaction at a personal level and being married or being in a relationship enables that. Knowing that there is someone with you, that can make you feel complete and spending the life with that person is a God's gift to all of us and the most natural thing to do in this age of technology.

Now that we looked at some benefits of being in a relationship, I would like to take us through my journey and some real-time experiences and learnings in my relationship.

Marriage is not a Fairy Tale

I got married (arranged marriage) to a wonderful man. I was looking forward to a happy married life. I thought my relationship experience will be very different than what I have seen in the past growing up. At that time, I had very high expectations about what my prince charming would do for any special occasion for me, how I will be treated extra special, how I will be the most important in his life, like a typical girl thinking of a happily ever after kind of married life. Guess What? Life is not a Fairy Tale, definitely not a happily ever after story for me, very soon I got a wake up call in the form of our first very bad fight. I was devastated, felt like I have fallen victim to marriage and relationship just like others. I felt I was lost, I was in lot of mental pain and it took me a few months to overcome that first bad experience I had in my marriage. The surprising fact was people around me including my parents seemed used to issues in relationship and the message was like always "this is nothing, every marriage will have issues honey, just make it work!"

So, I quickly realized I am not going to get help from anyone on this topic and also started believing in the message that these kinds of issues are expected and started to embrace the norm in the society. For the most part then on, we started to share some good interests and enjoyed many moments together, yet, every once in awhile we would have a disagreement and would end up having a heated dispute. My initial years in the marriage went like a roller coaster of good times and fearful tense moments. I would constantly question if I married the right guy, and why I am going through such pain and struggle with my relationship. From my husband's point of view, these issues were not a big deal, he would forget about an argument or he would just get mad at me for couple days and he would be fine after that. But I was taking on more than just getting upset. Time passed, we moved to

United States of America and started to make new friends, started new life, new job, it was exciting and a few years later we had our first baby.

Love at First Sight

I am not sure if you believe in love at first sight, but for me it really happened. I still remember that afternoon, I had fallen in love, Love at first sight, I was holding the love of my life in my hands. He is our first son, the nurse held this precious bundle of joy close to me as he cried while entering the world. I said hi baby, hi Vignesh baby, he immediately calmed down and was searching for the voice with his eyes closed. The fact that my voice, soothed a just born, newborn baby who was already recognizing my presence with his eyes closed and connecting with me just few moments after he came into this world made me cry tears of joy. I really felt like I have fallen in love, my heart was filled with joy and happiness, way more happiness I got in my entire married life till then. He is my first baby. We named him Vignesh Raj, Vignesh named after God of Wisdom and remover of Obstacles. I so believed in God Vignesh all my life that I wanted one of my own and named our Son. Like his name, my son Vignesh is always the remover of obstacles in my life. He brought so much joy and happiness that the relationship and other issues looked nothing and they faded away like he removed them for me.

With the arrival of our son, life has taken a different turn in my relationship. For couple years after my baby was born, life was all about him and enjoying his every single milestone and cherishing time with him. Reality started to kick in when responsibilities increased for me at work and other personal things not going very well. Once again, our relationship got into a mode of constant disputes, overcoming them and some very great times together, and more discussions. Every time we would have a discussion or disagreement and it wouldn't end very well, I would constantly go back into thinking why me, why I am going through this much suffering and pain. I took up too much on the emotional side and the only thing that would keep me going was Vignesh and my work. I made more friends and the more I started to understand my friends that were in a relationship, married, or married with young kids or married with kids grown up. Everyone I would speak to, everyone consistently talked about one or the other challenges they are facing in their relationship. I started to wonder if there is any family out there who has not gone through challenges. I did notice that families that are newly married and families with young kids especially more than one kid are the ones at edge of losing their marriage, or going through divorce in many cases. I always wondered why every relationship should go through rough times? what are some reasons couples fight? What is the impact on kids in the families going through relationship issues. I didn't want any of my personal life to impact my professional career not to mention work was very exciting (or maybe it was an escape for me out of this pain) and at one point in time I was working 60+ hours a week for couple years to excel in my career. I finished my Masters and took a few professional certifications and I was on fast track to leadership position in my company.

Few more years passed and I went through very rough times in my own relationship as well and I was constantly hearing from my family, cousins and friends going through as well worse times in their marriage reaching out to me for advice. Since I always was solving for my problems without making announcements, everyone in my family/friends reached out to me to know how I am Happy, and what guidance I could provide to them to make their life happy. To help them, and help me I started researching and learned a lot about human psychology and marriage and started coaching myself and couple of my close friends. Deep down I knew that, I was scared that if I do anything to take aggressive action with my friends or cousins relationship issues or even with my own relationship it will only make things worse, it would result in more fights, violence and maybe in divorce and those kids who are precious and innocent would end up with parents separated.

I was and I am still very against divorce. I do not believe that divorce is a solution unless in extreme cases of safety and violence or harassment. Most of the cases I have witnessed were lack of understanding, ego issues, lack of expressing love, lack of respect for spouse, lack of <u>relationship discipline</u>, financial issues, health issues, issues due to kids, parents (yes parents). I then started coaching women to think differently about the relationship problems, rather than complaining about the issues and their spouses, I would ask them some specific questions that would make them think differently. But I was only influencing only a few and only to an extent. Once they are back into their family life, things would flip back to the same.

Human Psychology is very unique to each individual and there are common patterns too. Below I am sharing with you my findings through tons of research I did, speaking to relationship coaches, speaking to experienced long married couples, young couples who are managing marriage well etc, about why couples disagree and fight to a point they grow apart.

All Couples Fight

I love this quote from Shakespeare, it changed my life longtime ago and so resonates with me in many aspects of life. There is a lot in this quote to learn.

Shakespeare said:

"I always feel happy, you know why? Because I don't expect anything from anyone. Expectations always hurt… Life is short, So love your life, Be Happy… & Keep smiling… just live for yourself and Before you speak, Listen, Before you write Think, Before you spend, Earn. Before your pray, Forgive. Before you hurt, Feel. Before you hate, Love. Before you quit, Try. Before you die, Live."

Every couple fights, in fact every human being fights/disagrees with others. That is human nature, unless you are extremely suppressed or completely shut down in expressing yourself.

There are many reasons why couples fight in marriage/relationship and my research tells, the various reasons can be categorized into fights/disagreements resulting from three main sources. I will also discuss some solutions to these if practiced well will help us fight less and love more.

Personnel: this includes different personalities in marriage, expectations from each other, trusting each other, personal space.

Expectations is the first enemy in marriage/relationship, expectations is like a slow poison causing the death to happiness. Marriage comes with many predefined expectations like, my wife will cook for me, my husband will buy me expensive gifts, my wife will look thin for ever, we will have great sex for ever, my husband will be the strong one emotionally, we need to be together all the time, my husband will cook, what I like is what he/she will also like, he/she will change for me, we don't need personal time, wife will always agree to husband, husband will always want to hang out with the wife, husband will help with kids, wife will help with laundry forever, husband will do trash, wife can stay home for good, husband doesn't get tired at all, wife knows exactly how to please the in-laws, husband will love wife's parents etc.

When couples enter marriage with these pre-defined expectations, they tend to get upset when and every time any of these expectations are not met, then starts the initial fights in marriage which when not course corrected will become a big problem resulting in marriage breakdown.

Also, no matter how much you know each other, any two individuals on this universe are not completely alike, which results in different personalities, different way of thinking, different likes and different dislikes. Wife may be able to hold a kid in one hand, phone on the ear, and cook with the other hand. It doesn't mean that husband can do all of these at the same time too. Husband can work long hours and come home, have a drink and still keep it calm not stressing about work. Which means, husband/wife can do things differently and might take different amount of time to do a task, might solve things differently.

Also, when couples get engaged or married, it comes with a pre-assumption that they will be hanging out together for every single moment/incident in life there on. This assumption is a killer in marriage or in a committed relationship. There should be times when the partners should have their own personal time. Just as much time we spend together, we should invest in spending on personal time too and that is perfectly ok to build a strong relationship. <u>It is OK to be away from each other for a little bit time, so you can be a together for-ever</u>. Small separations actually help revive the relationship and reignite the passion in the relation.

Finally, on the personal front, trusting each other is a key to a successful relationship and when there is suspicion in marriage, or lack of trust, it will boil up the other person especially when they are honest and will result in major fights. Trust is the foundation for the relationship and it should be built super solid strong from day one.

Financial: The second breaker in marriage is the MONEY matters!!!

This includes, wife/husband making significantly less money than the other, one of the partners making siloed financial decisions, spending habits of wife vs husband, one spouse not having a job, disagreement on idea of savings etc.

When it comes to finances in marriage there will be times when money controls your relationship for many reasons. Not having a job or only one spouse working can make the spouse earning money feel like they should make all the financial decisions as if it is their "hard earned money" however, the significant other can feel let down in this process. This can result in major clashes in marriage. Also, even when both have a job and earning at almost the same level, many financial matters result in fights, the idea of saving for a husband could be way different than the idea of savings a wife would have, one might like to invest in stocks, the other might want liquid cash in the savings account. One might like to enjoy life right now and spend all the money, the other might want to buy expensive items to enjoy life, one might want to spend money over his/her parents and the other may want to buy assets and spend zero money on anyone, one may want to donate all the money all the time, the list goes on about how couples can get into disagreements over finances. Money matters always are the driver for fights and break-up.

External: This includes our lovely children, parents (or in-laws), family (sister, brother, sister-in-law etc) and extended family/friends, external affairs etc

It is way too hard for two individuals to be compatible all the time and when a third or fourth person joins the ride, it only gets rough. That is the bottom line.

In the initial days of marriage there is "you, me and parents (yours and mine)" and it is not easy to keep everyone happy when they get together or even worse if everyone is living together. You have to be very light minded and super understanding to not get into disagreements/fights when things go unexpected and different opinions float around for every single decision. Often couples start living out by themselves once they get married or in many cultures as early as the dating starts.

And with the introduction of our lovely children, comes a huge responsibility to the wife/husband as parents. Now in your life it is "you, me, our child/children, my parents, your parents" etc. This is where the struggle with marriage gets even worse. Wife expects husband to equally take care of the child, husband thinks it's wife's thing to change diapers, wife expects husband to feed the baby in the nights and be happy about it (LOL) you know what I am talking about. Husband expects wife to take care of the baby all night and not be grumpy about it. Wife puts on pounds and husband has no clue why she is gaining so much weight and makes fun of her baby fat etc

And as kids grow there will be other areas that makes it hard for wife and husband to not fight. You spoiled him like that, you are too strict with her and now she became like that, you should spend more time with your son, dropping them to after school activities, concerned about their education, their friends and influences as they enter high school, college etc.

Also, in marriage due to many reasons, especially after the arrival of kids, there will be times when passion and romance can get into the back burner and one of the spouse is finding that romance or affection in another external person resulting in disengaged spouse, extra marital affairs, or even long-term extra marital affairs. It is typical of men to find an interim partner when wife is not he is not getting the importance and affection and care he was getting before the kids from his wife. One can say "well the wife is busy with the baby and kids and these are his kids too not just the mom's, there is no time for the poor wife to take care of the kids and attend her husband, why is it the wife's problem to take care of kids and not husbands or vice versa etc etc". The reality is the most important need of a human being is the significance or importance factor. When the husband or wife see that in a relationship that significance factor is decreasing in the form of kids, parents, friends or anyother means, there is a natural tendency to follow the new interests or passions and sometimes that interest can be working extra at work, immersing on computer, browsing net forever and social media, drinking, cigarettes, in that search is also when the extra-marital affairs pop-up. Any man or women with high morals and values will not want to cheat their partner, however it can happen when there is lost passion, feeling of love is lost, the man factor is not pleased in the house and someone else is providing that love and attention. Even it is for a moment mistakes like these tend to happen and are happening even more than ever with increased exposure to others via internet, work, increased demand for instant help, instant pleasure, satisfaction of ego, to hurt the other spouse and make them feel jealous. These issues can eventually lead to many major fights and making the relationship even worse, to even breaking up and divorce.

Bottom line is that there are many many many reasons for a couple to fight and many more reasons to breakup. In this fast-paced world, there is an easy chance for people to lose the essence of building a lasting relationship and nurturing it from the beginning to keep it strong and fulfilling. These days we don't need strong reasons to break up. Both wife and husband are equally educated, earn money and have the self-respect that they cannot compromise. This makes it easier for couples to think that life is better off without the partner they fell in love with or they chose to marry. Very Sad!!

The core of this book is not to teach how to manage and work through relationship problems, instead it is to make you crystal clear with Happiness and no matter what is happening in your life, you will be able to change that and take charge of your happiness and create a Happy medium around you forever by following the techniques mentioned.

That said, there are better ways to manage relationship successfully, if we understand the key value and manage it effectively than letting marriage manage us. So, how do we do it? It is by managing expectations to the most extent.

"In order to change your relationship, first change yourself", (Tony Robbins). The root cause to many problems in a relationship is the expectation a person has on his/her spouse. Having expectations is a good thing, however, expectations can also be a killer of passion and unconditional love in a relationship. The minute you start expecting, you are training your brain and heart to receive a certain response from your spouse and when the outcome is different you start to think that it is your spouse's fault that he or she did not meet your expectations.

So, are we not supposed to expect anything from our spouse/partners/kids? What is the point of relationship if we can't expect anything? If there are no expectations, where is the accountability? The answer is, yes you can have expectations BUT do not expect things to go your way, and expect the unexpected. How do we get to that stage where we do not expect things to go our way? How can we get comfortable to give up on expectations ?

The answer is to start training your brain to start looking at relationship/marriage as another member in your family "another element, a third element in your life". When you look at a married couple, you should get into a mindset of considering marriage as three people 1. the wife 2. the husband and 3. the marriage/relationship. And if we focus on our thought process and discussions around these three people, then our discussions will take a different outcome. So, when you and your spouse get into discussion or expectations mismatch, you need to start considering what is the effect on marriage because of this discussion and what impact it will have on the marriage. If we can give this marriage element a unique significance in our life and we start asking those questions, it will start to become a second nature to walk away from unnecessary discussions and building a more richer bonding in a relationship.

These are just some findings from my research on what can be done to reduce and leverage conflict in a healthy way. While doing this research, I have uncovered something even more powerful and impactful that had changed my life and many people's life, it has helped me be more strong and grounded and handle my life with passion, create long lasting joy and happiness. Each of us find this in different ways, some hit their rock bottom to find this, some need a breakthrough and determine their peace. It is <u>Purpose in Life</u>.

Finding one's purpose in life is a key element to finding happiness, happiness is a feeling and this feeling can be felt on a sustainable way only when you know your purpose and the work you do and the life you are living has a meaning and that meaning drives the inner strength that you need on a daily basis.

Breakthrough - Purpose in Life

After a few more years of fun and rough relationship cycles, we found out our second baby is on the way. I was in a high demanding role at work and having a second baby was not in our plans (typical career woman speaking here). I realized I need to get through this tough phase in marriage by myself. Work expectations were high, I was the only one earning in the house. My parents were very supportive and helped me during pregnancy and after the baby was born for a little time. This baby was high demanding baby, had colic, poor feeding and needed a lot more attention than others. Sleepless nights, crying baby, high demanding job, spouse who would help seldom made me lose my mind. We ended up having crazy fights and some of them were not even worth fighting for if I look back (Later I will mention about how husbands psychology changes after kids especially the second baby and more and what women can do to keep their sanity and the marriage safe)

Help came in the form of my mom who visited and stayed with me for few weeks after the baby was born. I still had sleepless nights with the baby, and full time job in the daytime and 2-3 hours commute every day. I was doing much better with my mom's help though. I called her back in few months when my husband had to travel abroad. Those were the best months after my second baby. I still had the same high demanding job, but I was able to manage everything very well, I lost about 30lbs and was eating healthy, did great progress at work, Got a new exciting position with larger leadership role. (Go to Leverage Help section to get some practical tips how and who to ask for help and not struggle alone, it's ok if when your spouse is not stepping up to help)

Suffering was at peak after my mom left, not much help at home and I was frustrated why people should go through the mental trauma and struggle to raise a baby and on top of it a rough relationship, all by themselves. I kept asking myself is there anyone out there to help people like me and thousands and probably millions out there going through rough relationship and needing help at difficult times? I didn't need someone to do magic or anything, all I was looking for was some dedicated real/virtual friend, a support system than one can rely on, and talk to openly about my relationship issues, someone who is passionate about solving such issues and is objective and they would make everything possible to make my relationship work. I was losing sleep thinking and thinking for a solution. Things got really worse with my relationship to a point where my basic principles of "give and take respect" and "never fight in front of kids" was broken many times. I have gone through tremendous pain, my heart was broken a zillion times now and added to that, there were many significant changes going on at work, which made a huge impact on my personal life as well. I was at the edge of separating from my spouse and something magical happened that triggered a spark and brought clarity on my purpose.

Be the Change I want to see in world (Mahatma Gandhi)

I still remember it was December 7th, it was about 2.00 AM, I didn't sleep all night thinking why I am going through so much humiliation, my husband told me things he should not have and I was in shock and thought to myself why am I putting up with my husband and our relationship. I asked God what did I do to deserve so much suffering.

I did not sleep that night. Next day was bad, I felt devastated. I felt overwhelmed with a full-time job, a baby that demands me to be with him every second and wakes up three times during the night and husband not helping at all with the baby. This time I was not able to distract my focus to anything for a long time. I would constantly come back to thinking what is the solution to end these fights for good in my relationship as well in many more families that will go through in future and/or are going through right now.

"The breakthrough moment"

Next night my older son came for a sleepover and he seemed very concerned that I was crying and sad for many days. I quickly tried to cheer myself up so he doesn't see me in this vulnerable state. He then asked me a dreadful question. The question that triggered a big jolt in my body and mind and thoughts and forced me to change the way things are in my life. He said something very simple yet powerful for me come out of the pattern of fights and negative thinking, he said,

"Mummy, are you and Daddy getting a divorce?"

That was one thing I never wanted to hear from my kids. I never wanted my kids to go through the uncertainty, that pain in the heart and fear in life, which I have experienced and hated growing up. I immediately told him "No". At that time, I didn't know what my husband was up to if he was thinking to separate, but something inside me told that I should make it work. I should change myself and get out of this state of constant fights over small things that don't matter in the larger scheme of life. I forgave myself and my husband and put everything behind me and decided "I will be the change I want to see in the world" like Mahatma Gandhi said.

I then immediately decided to make a difference in how relationship is looked at and provide the help that is needed to young couples and families out there to get over with some of the day to day expected issues in marriage. I started conditioning my mind to first implement some techniques in my own relationship and quickly started seeing the results. I continued to condition my mind, I surrounded myself with some great books and virtual mentors, which made a significant change in my mindset (I will later describe about mind conditioning techniques and its benefits in detail)

Purpose of my Life

I quickly realized, that God made me witness and go through and witness so much suffering and pain in my life and relationship for a purpose and gave me even more hard times in the form of my second child, tough husband, tough career, all the people reaching out to me for help and coaching for a reason. I realized my second child was born to show me the purpose in my life. I had become stronger, physically and mentally not just to deal with personal relationship issues, I was there to do more than just helping my own life. I am meant to "Become the Change I Want to See in the World". These words resonated with me day and night. On December 26th day after Christmas, I made a decision that I wanted to become that change to make people cherish relationship, I wanted people to see relationship differently than as a responsibility or as a mutual business or as a trade or as a burden or a struggle or a PAIN. As I digged through this mission, I found the real motivation and passion I have in life which is to see **everyone Safe, Self-sufficient and Happy**. And that is how my purpose in life, "Create a Happy Frame" took shape with a mission to end the epidemic of mental suffering and pain

Since then I have been conditioning my mind and soul to get centered with life and help myself and others in this path (refer to different phases of relationship and make an assessment where your relationship is and apply techniques that will work for your phase specifically)

In an instant I became a new person. I am now focussed on success and creating a proven actionable path to successful relationship. As I kept thinking more about this idea, everything started to fall in place. I continued to coach my friends and family members who are going through tough times. While I was discussing the new me with my friend, she shared with me her challenges and that she was going into a depressed state in her lifer due to her marriage and relationship. I really couldn't see her in that state and started helping her by conditioning her mind. Coached her to focus on issues as opportunities and introduced the concept of mind conditioning and helped her considering marriage as third element. She saw positive results. Another friend went through a rough marriage and with coaching, her confidence went up higher and she took on a new job and now working her way through her career, still working on her relationship, but she is out of her depressed state and moving on with her life. Since, then I have not stopped, I have coached a few more women now and helped them successfully build confidence back in them and helped them come out of their narrow thinking to clear up and thinking broad. My goal is to help every women and men out there to create more happiness and not let relationship or marriage kill happiness in life.

So, what is mind conditioning, why do we need to care about it and what are the benefits, Let's take a look!!

Mind Conditioning

I have read many books and many of them resonated a message strongly that "when you believe in yourself and train your brain to believe in it, then whatever your mind is up-to is going to be a reality". Tony Robbins wrote many books and every single book or video I watched conveyed the message of conditioning your brain one or the other way. Also, Jason Selk's "Executive Effectiveness" talks about how mind conditioning is so important in life to accomplish success. Many successful CEOs and successful leaders are now sharing publicly about their mind conditioning routines and benefits. Effective mind conditioning is very powerful, it can improve your emotional intelligence and help find your center and can take a person to the heights they can only imagine. In this book, I will focus on mind conditioning specific to building happiness in your life and improving your relationship primarily and we will come up with a plan that will include rest of the aspects your life as well. I highly recommend reading Tony Robbins "Awaken the Giant Within" and Jason Selk "Executive Effectiveness" for further details on applying mind conditioning to succeed in every aspect of your life. Mind conditioning is not completely a new concept. It is based of concepts of meditation. Most of the cultures either pray GOD or some higher power or practice meditation in one or the other form. When they do that they sit and close eyes and focus on the life events which to an extent is the concept behind mind conditioning.

Mind conditioning is a very important skill that everyone should develop in order to achieve success, peace and happiness in life. It is a way to train your brain and thoughts to enable the best possible solutions for an individual. Mind conditioning will make you fit emotionally and mentally. Just like you exercise your body to gain good health and fitness, mind conditioning is going to reap you the benefits of mental health and happiness. It is a very powerful exercise that can lead you to the path of happiness and success.

So, how will mind conditioning help relationship exactly, you must be thinking? we'll learn that in the next few pages. Before we can get into details of relationship mind conditioning, lets do some prep work (you need to identify your happy moments, what matters to you). I would like you to start thinking about life overall and do a self-check about yourself. I want you to think about how your life was before marriage/relationship and how it is after. I want you to think what is your strength or happiness factor before and after marriage. This self-check is very important to be able to assess the quality of life you deserve and the happiness you want to create for yourself.

Take a couple moments here and jot down on a piece of paper or in the space below about how life was before your relationship (what made you most happy, what made you sad, were you able to do something that you loved doing before marriage that you are not able to after, what is good about the current relationship, what is not so good about current relationship, what is the one sacrifice that you made due to your marriage that frustrates you and perhaps keeps you up at nights, is there something that bothers you about your marriage etc).

Good job!!! taking first step towards improving your quality of life. After completing this exercise and rest of the book, your life will change for good, your thoughts will change for good!! At least that is the intent of this book

Now, let's work on getting clarity on your needs in your life and relationship.

My life Before and After Relationship

In the template below write down what makes you feel happy and empowered and then put a check-mark or simply say yes or no against them in the before and after marriage columns to show if that element of happiness existed before marriage only or it is still in your relationship or after marriage.

Repeat the same process for things that make you unhappy. Only list the items as they are still relevant to you now and important to you now in this stage of your life. For example, eating ice-cream or playing video games, or pubbing probably was the most important and happy moment for you when you were a teenager, but you may not care for it as much now (I have filled out an example for better understanding.):

#	What gave me happiness	Before Marriage	After Marriage
1			
2			
#	What made me unhappy	Before Marriage	After Marriage

1			
2			
3			

Mind Conditioning Deep Dive

#	What gave me happiness	Before Marriage	After Marriage
1	Freedom - I was able to do what I like, and be how I like	No	Yes, I can be myself and I am not judged
2	Personal fitness and grooming	Yes	No - it's a struggle to get me time these days
3	I loved having friends and family visits, giving/receivin g gifts	Yes	No - inviting friends and company is a struggle and results in fights
#	What made me unhappy	Before Marriage	After Marriage
1	Too much responsibilities	No	Yes :(
2	Lack of love and care	No (lots of love from parents	No (I still have parents and my kids and

		and friends)	friends who love me a lots) can get more love and care from my spouse
3	Endless Childcare	No	Yes (Raising kids is a life time project)

Now take a closer look at the things that were making you happy, (from the example above) freedom to be yourself, hanging out with friends and family, fitness and grooming, giving gifts etc were giving happiness and most of these did not continue after marriage.

Also, on the other hand note that too much responsibility, endless childcare, lack of love and care are contributing to the unhappy side of the chart.

Great job on the exercise. If you did not, I would like you to take a few minutes and complete it and come back to rest of it. Please take time for this important step.

I will now take you a little more deeper into finding your center and to uncover your real happiness. Let's take a closer look at all the items that were giving you happiness for a moment. Are there any patterns, are there any special feelings you get when you think of those moments? I would like you to remember what was going on in your life when you had those happy moments. Who was with you, what were you doing, how does happiness feel to you? Do you feel full in your heart? does it make you excited thinking about those moments? are you feeling good right now thinking of those moments? can you make this feeling of happiness permanent? Yes you can, by implementing a powerful tool called Self Check.

What is Self Check, how do we perform a self check, let's take a look. In order for us to do a self check we need to think deep down our soul and tap into that special talent we have to open up. We need to retrospect our life and think about what has gotten us to where we are how we can get to where we really want to be. Doing a self check is crucial to finding your uniqueness and the gift you have that no one else has. There is no right or wrong assessment in a self-check. There is no particular time to do a self-check, its ideal you do it when your mind is fresh and away from possible distractions, early morning before rest of your family is awake or late night or in the afternoon when no one can distract you for sometime.

My SelfCheck

When I was a child, I was like most other kids, wanted many things to make me happy. Wanted new clothes, new toys, new books, new shoes and the list goes on. There was always something me and my sisters wanted, no matter how much we already received from our parents and family.

When I was a child, there was a personal trait of mine, which pulled me and made me extra interested about giving gifts to others. My family was low middle class and my dad was the breadwinner in the house, he used his money very effectively. He would spend majority of his money to send us to the best schools possible and we lived in best homes for a low middle class. Rest of it was second priority for him. We wouldn't get much pocket money or allowances to spend. I was about 8 - 9 years when it was my elder sisters birthday coming up, she is very special to me, even today, she is like my mom after my mom. I really wanted to buy her something and I knew she loved Lord Krishna. One day on the way to home while sitting in a public bus, I saw a statue of Lord Krishna they were selling on the road side. I thought immediately, that I should come back with someone and buy that for my sister. So, over the weekend, me and my cousin decided to surprise her with the present, I only had Rs.25 (about $0.5). We both rode our bike about 5 miles away to buy the present. The price was more expensive than the money I had, but we bargained and negotiated and somehow managed to get it (that was a miracle the man sold it for less than he can). On the way back my cousin was riding the bike and I was sitting in the back of the bike and we had a fall, which made a crack on the statue, I didn't give up. We went home and fixed the statue and the next day we gave it to my sister. She was pleasantly surprised, she was astonished that we went out of our way to get her this special present, we didn't get in trouble with our parents, she kept it secret. I spent all the money

I saved for months to buy her this present and I was still very happy. There was special feeling deep down my gut, and my heart felt full, when giving the present to her. I had that feeling almost every time I was giving a gift to someone. I always liked to initiate gift giving when it is someone's birthday or special occasion. I would sometimes not have the money to give the gift by myself, but I would initiate the idea and get a group to contribute and I would take on the task to go shopping. I would give my time to get the best deal and best gift for the person. At that time I did not realize that happiness is in giving. If I look back now and consider all the happy moments I had prior to marriage and after, I was into giving throughout my life, I gave presents, I gave time, I gave support (financial and mental) to my family and friends when needed and I gave birth to two wonderful sons and those were the moments of happiness in my life. <u>That is my Selfcheck around happiness and it came to</u>

clarity to me happiness is in giving and letting others give and not always in taking.

Prep Step 2:

Your Selfcheck

Retrospect moment: Can you stop reading further at this time and do your selfcheck with focus on your life. Think about how happy you were in the past, what are some of the moments of happiness as a child or teenager or young adult before your relationship or marriage and what was the reason behind your happiness?

What did you see in your happy moments? Did you see any significant moments when someone gave things to you, someone loved you, gave you new clothes, gave you a gift, gave you surprise etc and how did you feel when you received things. Now also think about when you gave things to others, you gave gifts, you gave your time, you gave birth, you gave a hug, gave a surprise, helped someone in trouble, helped someone in need, donated your clothes and how did that feel to you? Most of the human nature think that, ideally receiving things makes people happy. However, studies and my personal experiences including have proved that receiving things only make you happy at the moment or a little longer and then we forget about that moment. Is that true for you? would you remember your dad giving you a toy for your birthday more than if you went out of your way shopping and bought a gift for your dad, which surprised him tremendously? Do you remember your mom giving you love when you were a child more or do you remember you giving love to your baby? When you give things, that satisfaction, gratitude, strength, that going out of our way to make it special for others stays with you forever. Those are the special moments in your life that you cherish for long time and the moments that makes you special out of rest of the people around you. Every person in this world has this special gift in us, and one of it is the gift of being able to give. We don't have to be rich or super smart or have lots of money to give, we are already giving one or the other way already. It is just that we are not thinking that we are giving. Giving is so powerful and it plays an important role in your marriage too.

In order to have a successful relationship, one or both of the partners should be willing to give in. Giving will not only make you happy but it will also make you great. Giving in a relationship will make you achieve greatness in your relationship. In order to be able to give into your relationship, you should really realize the value of the relationship to keep it together and to nourish it. When there is such a clarity in a relationship, then the day to day conflicts and disagreements won't make any negative impact on the relationship. It will rather replenish the relations to next level.

There is a part in each of us that is a giver, at one or the other point in time, we must have given our money or our time, or our love to someone. It is about time to nourish that giver in you to change your relationship for good. The fact that you are reading this book tells me that you are not anyone who would give up. This book will show you how you can train your brain to be the giver in the relationship than just being the receiver. When it comes to relationship, everyone enters into the relationship with lot of expectations and dreams of a bright future with their spouse and expect a smooth ride with no bumps or detours in the way. No one specifically invests in time and money to understand relationship and what to expect in a relationship and not to mention if there are issues, what are the kinds of issues that arise and forget about how to solve those issues. There is a lack of awareness in the general public about relationship and the downsides of not creating our stories and mindset to meet the new chapter in our lives.

Prep Step 3:

Change your Mindset to Focus on Solutions

Talking about problems will not solve problems, talking about solutions will solve problems. Shift your focus and shift your life. ~Tony Robbins

Look at problems as an opportunity to strengthen your relationship not to weaken it. ~ RR

Regardless of how many problems we face in a marriage, except for very few that are tied up with violence, every other problem is solvable and relationship is something we can sustain if we want to. Often in relationship or marriage people breakup thinking there are better options out there for them than the one they are currently in. Let me tell you the reality of life. The better option out there is very dependent on how you think about yourself and the option is for you. So, no matter what life brings on to you, if you are looking for better option all the time, there will not be anything or anyone that will meet your needs. The point I want to make is that, options are there for everyone, but that doesn't mean what you have is not the best option, it probably is the best option if you look at it with the right perspective, right respect and right love that you would give to your best option in your mind.

Research shows that every problem has a solution one or the other way. It is our thinking that makes a problem unsolvable, bigger than it is, painful than it is and emotional than it is. For example when a husband says, he can't play with the kids, the wife can think of it as bigger problem that the husband doesn't want to play because he doesn't love her as his wife and so he doesn't love her kids and so, he doesn't think that he should play with them. Whereas the real response from the husband is that he simply cannot play at that time. He might be busy wrapping up work, or has to color his hair or iron his clothes or simply need to go to the bathroom.

The exaggeration of a situation can many times bring up more problems we have than we can solve for. Again going back to basics of training our mindset and thought process to not make a problem bigger than it is and remove the emotional attachment of it will help us solve many problems easily without causing much pain at all.

Problem Scenario 1:

Husband comes home after a busy day at work and probably driving for more than an hour in bad traffic. Wife is at home all day with kids and waiting for husband to get home and help. Husband will not be in a state to help, the wife will not be in a state to not get help and guess what will happen ? in a normal world, there will be a small or a big fight about why husband can't help as he is already tired making money for the family, wife is disappointed that kids are just her responsibility and the husband just works and does nothing else. So, do you see how the big fights start ?

However, if we think of marriage as another significant part of the family and respected its value, then we can start to think differently. If one of the partners in the marriage can think about what is this fight going to do to our marriage or relationship ? Is this fight worth a big dent in our marriage ?

Imagine going through the problem scenario mentioned above every single day, it will quickly make you a different person than you are prior to your marriage and in your early days of marriage. It will make you a wife who is yelling at your spouse, a husband beating up your wife due to lack of patience and control of anger. It will make you a mom who is whining all day with kids instead of enjoying them. It will make you a dad who will never have time to read a story to a little one. You know what I am talking about. You definitely can put an end to these day to day small problems. With a little bit of planning and prioritizing where we spend our money it can help solve for a longer relationship you deserve. Implement the solution steps and focus on solving the problem rather than creating new problems out of a small solvable problem.

Solution for the above problem scenario: Look into solving couple things here:

1. Manage Expectations:
    a. Expect the working spouse to be unavailable for x number of hours everyday and respect the value they are adding to the company or business they are working for and to the world.
    b. Expect staying home spouse to be exhausted of taking care of the home and kids and other items around the house.
    c. Expect that anger and frustration will only make things worse.
2. Solve the real problem:
    a. If the spouse is always tired getting home from work, look at, if the work is too stressful that he/she can't leave it out the door and spend quality time with family. Help find another job closer to home, or less stressful role, or open your own

business that makes more sense and you enjoy working hard at.

b. If the kids or household chores are draining your spouse's energy and passion for your relationship, get help in the form of a daycare/nanny/babysitter to help with kids even for few hours a day/week

c. Spend sometime together weekdays without kids. Go and meet your spouse for dinner/shopping/movie after work and come back home together.

Problem Scenario 2:

Wife is the primary breadwinner in the house, working many long hours at work to keep up with work expectations, stay at home husband who expects wife to come home take care of kids, do all the cooking cleaning etc. In addition to that what happens if husband starts having some bad habits like excessive drinking, gambling away hard earned money? what will happen if this behavior continues for a month, a year, few years? in a normal world, there will be many fights about why husband can't help as he is staying at home, why is he drinking too much, why does he like to gamble away hard earned money and that too earned by the wife ? There goes another marriage breaking fight series.....

Let's look at this problem keeping in mind that marriage is a significant part of the family and has highest value. If one of the partners in the marriage can think about what is this fight going to do to our marriage or relationship? Is this fight worth a big dent in our marriage? Do we want to crash our marriage vehicle just because we are going through a hard phase in life?

Applying our solution focused relationship techniques rather than problem focused and see the wonders it can make on marriage and your relationship.

Solution for the above problem scenario: Look into solving couple things here:

1. Manage Expectations:
    a. Expect the working spouse let it be wife or husband to be unavailable for x number of hours everyday and respect the value they are adding to the company or business they are working for and to the world.

    b. Expect staying home spouse may not like to be a stay home spouse and is depressed in thoughts of how to get out of the house and so will not be capable of taking care of kids or cooking/cleaning like the traditional stay at home spouse would. They may indulge into bad habits to keep you away from expecting them to taking care of something they don't like.

c. Expect that anger and frustration will only make things worse, fighting and thinking why me? why now ? why can't he step up or why can't she do everything and don't complain about it ? this kind of complain focused mindset will not help.

2. Solve the real problem:

a. If the stay at home husband is not willing to take care of kids or cook or clean like a traditional stay at home spouse would, then look into what is the real issue. Is his ego of being the man of the house is constantly broken if he is cooking or cleaning and taking care of kids ? Is he drinking with depressed thoughts that he is unable to make money for the family and his wife is working hard to earn money ? Is he gambling away the money thinking he can make some money in the process so he will have his own spending money ?

b. The point I want to make is, there will be an underlying reason why people act the way they act, if we can make an effort to understand rather than complain about it, we can fix the root cause than the symptom of the problem.

c. Once the, root cause is found which in the case above was the male ego being hurt to do household chores while wife is working, take an action to eliminate that problem. Try to find a job that will help him, be creative, maybe he can go to school to learn new skills to get a job, look at more than one option to keep him engaged, make him join a sports club where he gets some personal time and makes new friends and new network. Get him out of the house. In this process if you have to spend more money to hire a babysitter or ask family to help with caring for kids etc, please do because nothing is more important in your life than your wife/husband relationship and definitely not money.

Go ahead and write down one of the problems you are facing in your relationship and think about what is one thing you can do right now to make the situation better with focus on solutions?

_____

_____

_____

_____

_____

Let me share with you one of the problems one of my friends faced in her marriage which could have resulted in a marriage break-up and happiness killer in many other families. We solved the issue with a focus on solving the problem vs inflating the problem.

This is how she exactly explained to me:
"He almost killed me today with a 15 pound weight, he almost hit me with it. He gets angry and cannot control himself when I confront him with anything. Why am I not reporting him? This happened a few times now, ever since my next baby news came up, I am like a most hated person for him. He doesn't love me anymore, and he doesn't want to care for the kids.... what do I do, break up with him and live my life without him??? ". I Love this lady, very sweet. I really wanted to do something for her and help her. We worked together to look at the real

99

issue. What is causing all the problems for them. Is the solution to break up will solve her problems? What is she happy with? I went through a deep exercise with her (details of which I am not sharing here for privacy reasons) and getting her into the mindset of solving the real problem vs the symptoms of the problem.

This friend of mine didn't break up, instead she took this opportunity to change herself for good. Rather than complaining about her husband and asking questions why she is in the problem state that she is today, she took a different route. She decided to train her brain to see the solutions to the problems in her life, than problems themselves. She changed her outlook to life. She started thinking and tried to understand what made them get to the state they are in marriage from the state they once were enjoying each other's company, made love, watched movies, had endless nights, playing games etc. As a result of this exercise, it was clear to her that the arrival of kids and other responsibilities and change in expectations of her husband definitely not only made them apart, made them strangers of each other's feelings. Two strangers living in the same house and not able to find time to know each other. She slowly looked at all the areas that have caused her pain, and to her surprise it was not her husband who was at fault many times, it was also her who was trying to be perfect and killing happiness in her life while constantly comparing her life to her other friends and family members which caused her more pain than what her husband was doing to her. She also realized that she had done many things that triggers her husband's ego and circumstances to follow. This whole process took her about a few months. It was worth doing it. She shared, "Now I exactly know how I can deal with many issues in my life. I have freed myself from wrong expectations and I understand my husband way better and support him and help him during difficult times.

He has more respect for me and we are not strangers any more. It's a work in progress!!"

She implemented many solutions and able to successfully drive her relationship with her husband and kids. Since then, I haven't heard any incident when they both had another major fight or even a heated dispute, they do get into discussions and she knows exactly what to do and how to drive the discussions constructively. What helps her every time is her thought process of a happy frame (which I will explain in detail in the next few pages). Her comparison of her husband and her married life to that of others doesn't impact her anymore.

To tie things together forever, I helped her to identify what her purpose in life is. She started exploring to understand this concepts and diving into finding real purpose in her life. Definitely her life purpose was not just having kids and a loving husband and nice luxuries to enjoy. Finding a purpose in her life tremendously helped her out on the days when things would not go as expected or planned.

Finding purpose in life is very important. Do you know what is your purpose in life? On what mission are you on? What do you want to change in this world? Whom do you want to help? What keeps you up at nights? What problem frustrates you that you want to change it or eliminate it?

Find your Purpose in Life

Thank you for being with this book so far. We have come long ways with respect to managing relationship successfully and reduce the amount of conflicts by focusing on the solution side.

Now that you have solved a time-consuming relationship problem task (fights and dealing with the emotional drain due to the fights in relationship) in your life, you definitely should have more free time. Now, do not use all your time to spend on internet browsing gossip, stocks, facebook, twitter, instagram, spa, shopping or running errands all day. Instead, carve out some time even 15 minutes out of your day to think about how you can serve the community around you. Sit down and think about what keeps you up at nights and what is that one special thing you want to solve in the world to make a difference? Think about your purpose in life. Everyday make time to sit down peacefully and write down your thoughts about your purpose in life and how you can give back, soon you will come to the realization of a passion inside you which was sleeping due to lack of inspiration from you. Bring that passion to life, feed that passion with some creativity, now get on Google and search for information to engage you in this new found passion and you will see a new you, who is not just about Taking, the new you is also about Giving back to the community and to your relationship. The new you is larger than yourself and can make a positive impact in your relationship and in the world. When you get into the Giving mode, your view at the relationship is very different than before. Do you agree?

You are not about just yourself anymore, you are now pumped up with a passion to change your relationship and life. However, there will be a stage when your daily tasks will clutter your drive and put it to an end. So, you need to develop a dedicated routine to keep that positive relationship going for good. Below are some steps to condition your mind and stay focused on helping your relationship to a new phase for good.

By going through this exercise, I identified my purpose in life. I feel more centered and stable and more empowered than anyone, ever since I have uncovered my purpose in life.

Social Status Stigma

There are many men and woman out there struggling to manage expectations of marriage or relationship. The culture around us puts us in a situation where we have certain amount of pressure to keep up with the society to prove to others, that we are happy or we are up to the mark with others etc. All those postings on social media like Facebook, twitter, watsapp, instagram etc "hey we bought a new house", "our kids are going to an expensive private school", "we bought a luxury car", "my spouse bought me an expensive ring", "we have the coolest kid", "we are going on a fancy vacation", etc are indirectly and passively putting pressure on others to feel sad about their relationship, creating a constant comparison framework and in this process the meaning of our real purpose of life is left uncovered and unexplored. I have heard from many of my friends and family that they had to delete facebook from their phone and not use it to wean away from such information.

During one of my trips to India few years ago, I have uncovered how much pressure young couples are going through to meet or exceed expectations of the society. One of my friends told me that, there is a strong need to maintain a certain social status in their community so that they are treated with respect and love from their friends and family. They are required to send their kids to expensive schools just because the schools are affordable by rich communities only. Throw a birthday party spending lakhs of rupees of money, or thousands of dollars and buying expensive jewelry for their spouses and kids. Drive expensive cars and If they cannot do that, then they wouldn't meet the social status. Young couples are struggling to earn money only to spend it and show off to their families that they are rich, when in reality they are faking it and making up for it later. Ending up with false pride and huge credit card debt.

I also noticed that many young men in their 20s and 30s newly married or married with young children are becoming addicted to alcohol, spending more than they can afford and partying excessively part of meeting social status. These men after consuming excessive alcohol then behave very mean and abusive to their wives and kids many times and to their parent or friends as they are under the influence of alcohol. I was particularly concerned seeing young couples with good professions getting side tracked in their life and doing things that are impacting their relationships in a bad way. They have zero social responsibility and are focused to make their own personal wealth by whatever means and get pleasure out of showing others low.

So, the question I often get is what can we do to help us come out of this social status stigma and help couples and families lead their relationship in a happier without sabotaging the real essence of a marriage and partnership? Is there anything that we can do prevent our families and friends from falling into this trap of showing off your status, becoming sad or depressed about comparing us to others and never being satisfied with what we already have? Does it mean we walk away from social media like facebook, twitter, instagram, watsapp and other social networking tools to make us silo from this world? No we don't have to walk away from anything.

There is a solution that will work always, again revolving around mind conditioning and I will tell you how you can be happy in your relationship while still engaging yourself with rest of the world.

Create Your Happy Frame

I did tons of research about why couples fight in a relationship and like I have mentioned in the earlier section of the book, external factors and expectations play a significant role in the relationship making or breaking. When a wife compares herself to another woman who is pretty and thin and tries to think that being pretty and thin is her happy frame and thinking that everyone likes people who are thin and beautiful, will make her life miserable if she cannot get to that level of body weight or external beauty.

When a man is comparing his wife to be a person who will do nothing but follow his instructions and agree to all his commands without using her brain or without sharing her opinions. "Look at Mark's wife, she does all the work in the house, cooks nice meals and takes care of the kids all day without complaining, so what is your problem doing it? He is then making his life miserable as well as his wife's by putting wrong expectations on his relationship and his wife. Another most common reason many married women get into a depressed state in a relationship is by building unrealistic expectations from their husband, that husband is the one that should provide for safety and security for her and her kids, failing to realize that sometimes the wife should also step up and take ownership of providing for safety and security for the family, this is a mindset shift from the traditional thinking.

The serious problem more than chasing after wrong expectations is that many times we don't even realize we are making our lives miserable with these unrealistic expectations.

I would like to now introduce the concept of "Happy Frame". Happy Frame is a powerful concept to eliminate the unrealistic expectations we set for ourselves and our partners and people around you and bring those expectations to a reality check, balance it with what is realistic and sustainable long term to create a Happy You and define Your Happy Life

Coming up with your own happy frame is very important in life and as well as in your relationship. In order for you to come up with your happy frames, you should understand and embrace that every relationship will have its own unique success criteria, constraints which contribute to their unique happy frame. In other words, there is no one size fits all and Happiness is unique to each individual. The couple should come up with the frame that fits their situation and embrace it. When you're happy frame is clear to you and you are proud to accomplish it, you will be self satisfied with your relationship and life overall day in and day out. When you are in your Happy Frame, the external factors cannot influence you to become sad or depressed about your relationship or life. Part of your happy frame should be things that are important for you and should make you feel special and loved.

So how to come up with your Happy Frame? I have broken it down into three simple steps which I will take you through in detail to accomplish it.

My ask of you is for you to spend a few minutes of quality time on this exercise and come up with your "Happy Frame" If you need a break at this point, please take a break and come back fresh to sit through it with full focus and attention

Create Your Happy Frame

Step1: Change your mindset, clear all barriers and embrace reality

It is OK for you as well as others to be HAPPY. Focus on the Good!!!

A. It is ok for you to be happy as well as others to be happy, take pride enjoying others happiness. So, when you see postings on social media about your friends and family sharing happy moments, focus on the good, and be happy for them and just BE HAPPY for them and STOP there. Don't get into comparison mode with others (Read Step 2 how not to compare to others)

B. This doesn't mean that you spend rest of your free time on facebook/twitter adding comments and following people's happy moments. There should be moderation to everything. Don't go overboard with anything.

C. Just by being happy for someone gives you a good feeling and fills your heart with warmth for others. Happiness creating endorphins release into your body when you feel happy and thankful so use this to your benefit.

Create Your Happy Frame

Step2: **Be your own comparison**

A. DO NOT compare yourself or your relationship to others, your relationship should be special and unique to yours. By comparing your relationship to others you are not only losing control of how to manage your relationship, you are adding unnecessary confusion to your expectations.

B. Do not expect your relationship to be praised by others. Don't expect your parents or friends or family to give kudos to you about how your relationship is going. Enjoy your relationship as is. Take pride in the efforts you are putting in your relationship.

C. Do not let others make you feel bad about your relationship. Nobody has a right to directly or indirectly look down on others relationship. It is your relationship. Take complete ownership. Be your own benchmark. If anything, give back some of the lessons learned or success stories to others as long as it is received well.

Create Your Happy Frame contd..

Step3: **Create your Happy Goals**
Task out your three Very Important Relationship Goals – Happy Goals in your marriage/relationship

A. What are the three important things that should work well for you in your marriage ex: Do you want your husband to give you a hug everyday? Do you want your wife to make you a morning coffee? Do you want your husband to express love by offering gifts? Do you want a date night every week? what ever those three things are to you in your relationship write them down and share them with your spouse. The sooner you come up with these goals the better it is for your relationship.

B. Align to how these three important things will be met in your relationship. You should be flexible how these three goals will be met. In other words, your goal could be to send kids to the best schools. That doesn't mean your kids should be going to the most expensive schools, instead it can be accomplished by giving them best education, moving closer to an area where public schools are best, or providing online tools etc, to leverage best education.

C. Combine your and your spouse's goals into a total of three Very Happy goals. Each goal should have a value clearly stated why it is very important and how it will make you happy in the relationship.

Once you have your three Very Happy Goals, frame it and put it up in a place where you see them daily at least once. Remember them during your "Happy Frame mind conditioning" (explained in the next section) routine to clearly identify and protect your Happy Frame. Have a quarterly checkpoint to see if your goals are meeting your values for the relationship and revise them as applicable. The revised goals should make you even more passionate about your Happy Goals even more than before.

Below are the templates. You can jot down your ideas and draft them, you can download the templates also from www.rajitharupani.com

Creating your Happy Frame is for you to get super clear about what YOU are and who YOU are, what makes YOU Happy and building the strength around yourself which is unique to you and is not colored or influenced by the others around you, including what journey your relationship or marriage is going through. Your Happy Frame will make you feel special, important, significant and you are the only one who has complete control of keeping it Happy and creating an abundance of Happiness.

So, without any delay....

Use the space below and....

"Create Your Happy Frame"

My Happy Frame

Our Relationship Happy Frame

Happy Frame - Mind Conditioning

Now that you have your Happy Goals defined and framed them, your Happy Frame needs to sit in your mind and you need to envision it every day so you can work towards to making it a real success. Happy Frame mind conditioning is detailed below, the concept is inspired from Ancient Indian Meditation principles and Praying concepts, Jason Selk's Mind Conditioning and Tony Robbins famous NAC - (Neuro Associative Conditioning and many other books and online articles)

Exercise:

1. Step 1: Breathing in and out for 12 seconds - Close your eyes and take a deep breath in for 5 seconds, hold it for 2 seconds and breathe out slowly for 5 seconds

2. Step 2: Your Happy Frame Vision - 30 seconds - **Keeping your eyes closed, visualize "Your Happy Frame" how you want to feel in your happy/ideal state of your relationship/marriage. It should be developed to align with what you want your relationship with your spouse, kids etc to be**

Example: My Happy Frame vision, I came home from work, looking very happy and accomplished, my husband was home already and gives me friendly gaze as I enter the family room, he seems happy to see me. He then congratulates me on a job well done, and he seems excited to share something interesting about his new venture. My sons in the age around of 12 and 5 look happy to see me, my older son gives me a hug and talks to me about how he had an interesting day at school and a new idea he is thinking about. I go to my younger son and give him a kiss, he seemed happy to see me home. He is looking happy and enjoying his pre-school days. Me and my husband are talking about our next trip and the donations coming up and how we can organize the trip to visit all the places to visit to donate to women and children in need. I am feeling happy and fulfilled, I am living my purpose. I am living my dream.

3. Step3: Life Purpose Vision - 20 seconds - Now continuing to close your eyes and vision the purpose of your life, what is that you want to have in life, what is that you are made for and how do you see yourself in the next 5 - 10 years. Visualize yourself in the future. Are you the one wanting to spend more time with your family, big house, great fame, serving the community, thinner you. Whatever is your desired state, visualize it in a positive way so the image of your future is clear and

motivating to you and has a strong meaning to you.

4. Step4: Breathing in and out for 10 seconds. Continue to close your eyes and take a deep breath in for 5 seconds, hold it for 2 seconds and breathe out slowly for 5 seconds

Now Open your eyes after the exercise. Repeat this exercise every day ideally after you wake up and before you jump into any daily activities. Try to do this exercise in the afternoon and in the night. Three times a day in the beginning to see a dramatic change in your mindset and relationship. The key is for you to believe it and do it with all your focus and heart.

5. Step 5 (optional): Enter Journal - 2 mins - This is a nice to do step to see yourself progress. Write one thing you did good yesterday and one thing you want to

continue and one thing you want to improve on today.

Protect YOUR HAPPY FRAME

Below are some additional tools to help you keep your Happy Frame Happy.

Do's and Dont's in a Relationship

Below are some things we can and cannot do in our relationship. Often times, we end up doing some things in our marriage or relationship and then realize if there was a checklist that told me what are some things not to do in a marriage and some things we should do to keep it strong. The below information is an attempt to help everyone in relationship or marriage to use as a quick reference, if we can or cannot certain things:

Do's in a relationship:

1. Do Smile. Smiling and laughing creates a positive energy in your relationship and eases any hardship you are going through. Smile every day as often as you can.

2. Do Kiss and Hug. Physical touch goes long way in a relationship, give your spouse a kiss and a hug every once a while. Dont think what they will think about it. it will always work. Even when you are unhappy about something, just giving a hug will fix it all. Just Do It!!

3. Do Appreciate. Appreciate your spouse the way they are and appreciate all that they are doing to make your relationship a success. Even if they are not doing anything but living with you, that itself is a significant thing to appreciate.

4. Do Respect. Often we get carried away with the craziness of busy lives filled with day to day activities and get into a mode of dis-respect to our spouse. Just because you are earning doesn't mean you deserve more respect than your stay at home spouse. When you realize that each of you are significantly important in a marriage is when mutual respect is possible. Don't get into a mode of

criticizing each other even for fun, it will end up becoming a daily routine and cause friction and damage.

5. Do Trust. Trust is an important factor in relationship. Spend enough time to understand your spouse and your relationship. Then build your trust around the understanding, there should be strong trust established to make a relationship successful.

6. Do have Fun. Life is full of unexpected events. You never know when it is your last moment. Every person is going through some struggle in one or the other way. Relationship should not be a struggle; it should not be a painful experience to anyone. Doesn't matter what stage you are in your life, have fun, live in the moment, do things to cherish and bringing good memories.

7. Do Exercise. Exercise is proven to improve your well being over all. Exercise relieves stress, improves energy levels, brings

positive mood, helps improve your emotional well being, helps control your body weight and improves your overall self confidence. You are a more happier person if you exercise for at least 30 mins a day.

8. Do Help. Running a relationship successfully is a very stressful task. Just because you are married doesn't mean your relationship is on auto pilot mode and doesn't need any navigation. Help each other out in your relationship and become the influencing partners to navigate your relationship to the desired destination safely!

9. Do find Solutions. Problems are everywhere, however if you are with the right mindset, there is a solution for every problem. When you become solution focused, then problems look very small and easy to deal with. You and your spouse will enjoy a more relaxing relation in this process. Take a moment to become

solution oriented as opposed to exaggerating problems.

10.   Do Listen. Don't be the talker in the relationship. Often times, one or the other spouse speaks a lot which shuts down your partner's excitement or thoughts that they also want to share. Stop for a moment and listen to your spouse, even if it hard to listen slow down and listen to hear the other perspective.

Don'ts in a relationship:

1. Don't argue for more than a couple minutes - in this day of age it is super easy to get into a discussion very easily, we can argue for no reason sometime. Sometimes we argue for personal interests or even for emotional reasons. JUST GET OUT of the discussion. DONOT entertain a heated dispute for long

2. Don't exaggerate - when there is a problem in the relationship, do not inflate and make the problem bigger. Don't add extra emotions or stories to the current problem and make it bigger than it can be.

3. Don't expect your way - many times the best thing to do is let go of your ego and control freak attitude and embrace different way of doing things. Learn to enjoy and be flexible with the way things work out. You should be focused on the what is the end goal and the impact to your relationship.

4. Don't assume - it is very easy to not have patience and take things for granted. Often we just make some assumptions that may turn into a problem. It is always good to let your partner know what you are assuming or ask if that is a good assumption so that there is no confusion of what is being expected.

5. Don't worry too much - Life is too short, don't spend your valuable time and your loved one's time with worries. There is no problem in the world that will get resolved successfully by worrying more about it. By worrying about anything too much you are not going to resolve the problem. Worrying will cause unnecessary mental drain and will make you lose confidence. Instead spend time constructively to find solutions rather.

6. Don't get too emotional - Emotional Intelligence plays a vital role in your relationship and in your life. Getting too emotional for everything is a sign of

weakness to deal with issues. There may be many times in a relationship that you are crying for every small issue, and throwing an emotional fit, I call it drama. Although drama is good to an extent to watch in movies, in real life drama can ruin your relationship. Constant drama will kill the passion and intimacy in a relationship

7. Don't focus on Problems - Can't stress enough on this one. There are problems everywhere. The way to look at problems is by thinking of it as a challenge and take up the challenge with full force. Win the challenge and celebrated it. There is no relationship problem that is humanly impossible to solve in my eyes.

8. Don't nag - nagging is the diabetes of relationship. It is a silent killer of bonding you build in your relation. If there is something that bothers you in your relationship, then discuss once productively and make a decision as to

what you and your spouse are going to do about it and take that action decided.

9. Don't make excuses - if there is a problem in your relationship, don't makes excuses why you cannot address it with your spouse or take an action to resolve it, don't blame your spouse for the issues in the marriage, don't get into a finger pointing mode for each others mistakes. When mistakes happen, admit it and take ownership to fix the root cause of the issue.

10.   Don't be scared - It is a must and should in a relationship that the couple will have a fight many times. Dont be scared to get into a relationship thinking about the whole conflicts and arguments and the mental stress that comes as a baggage with relationship. Rather consider conflicts as stepping stones to improve your problem solving capabilities. Take pride in managing your relationship successfully through the ups and downs of conflicts and happy moments.

11.   Don't be bossy - Inequality in a marriage will cause many problems, don't get into a mindset that husband is more than the wife or vice versa. No matter what your individual physical strength or financial strength or beauty or fame is, doesn't mean your partner or spouse is of less value. Only when you value each other equally and love each other as is, and not trying to control one another to do things your way, the relationship engine will run smoothly for long-term.

Tips for Husbands - Women's way of thinking

Dealing with women is an interesting topic. Women not necessarily are always looking for materialistic things all the time. They work hard just like men, they are constantly multitasking and trying to solve everything they can and are frustrated when things don't move fast enough for them or move their way. Many times all they need from you is for you to recognize and appreciate their work. Sometimes all you need to do to please her is give her a compliment about how good she is taking care of the house, or how appreciative you are about her taking care of the kids, or taking care of daily chores, doing a great job at work, doing a great job helping parents, others etc.

When asked how am I looking, instead of saying, "you look as usual" just tell her "You look beautiful". It means a lot when you give a compliment clearly to a woman than to tell them they look the same (even though in the husband's mind he is probably thinking she looks beautiful as usual and there is no difference when he says "you look the same" it doesn't make her happy a bit.)

Instead of asking "Did you clean the house today ?" just tell her "Thanks for cleaning the house" even if the house looks messy to you. Housework bogs down women more than anything, housework is never ending, imaging you doing work all day and it is never complete and doing the same work over and over for years all day. Women spend a lot of time trying keep things organized. By the time husband comes home it is possible that there might be things messed up. That doesn't mean she did not work on the house at all, infact she might be super tired of taking care of it all day so your comment or compliment can make her or break her mood dramatically. Sometime not saying anything can also trigger her emotions.

Instead of saying, "Your parents" just tell her "Uncle Aunty" it means a lot to her when you try to accept and respect her parents as you would respect your parents. Even if you disagree and dislike your in-laws keep a balance to show how much you dislike them. There is nothing you will accomplish by being disrespectful to her parents. You will only get a payback from her with similar attitude towards your parents if anything or to your kids or your relationship.

Instead of saying, "You look fat" just tell her "You look amazing". Seriously, thin or fat shouldn't matter to you in your relationship unless your wife is making money for you for being a model who needs to be thin to make money. Please think beyond looks. It is the nature of the person that should really matter than the looks. Now, if you really care for her looks in terms of her health, then you better help her maintain a good physique by encouraging her to go to the gym or some fitness class or program to keep with her health and physique.

Send compliments her way, doesn't have to be expensive gifts, simple text message, a phone call, a chocolate (I am super happy when mine gets me my favorite dairymilk chocolate), a juice, a kiss, a coffee anything small can definitely bring smile to her face. Tell her you like when she smiles.

Give her a hug and a kiss when possible. They need to know you like kissing her or giving a hug not when you need something from her or not just when you need to make love to her but otherwise too. Physical touch get two people closer beyond many kinds words can. Take time to kiss her thank you, kiss her bye, kiss her good job. Treat your lady with love and she will give back an abundance of love as a return gift.

Pamper her, One of my friends said, "my husband would pamper me by indulging me in chocolates and used to give me fruit facials at home in early days of our marriage. I was feeling like a princess and those were the best times in our marriage, when we would get quality time together and share each others stories while doing facials. He doesn't do that anymore, now that we have kids and too many tasks at hand", she said very sadly. Make your woman feel extra special every once a while. Doesn't have to be super expensive or time consuming. It can be simply bringing home her favorite chocolates, could be taking her to her favorite restaurant, buying her that special phone she has been waiting for, getting her a new outfit, any thing that you can express clearly to her that you love her and she is special to you in your life is going to make her feel on top of the world.

Know their weakness and help them. Wives get furious when her man doesn't answer her phone call or message. When men are irresponsible. When he forgets to do things that she asked to help with. When you ask them to repeat things. These are either high expectations or can also be considered as weakness that wife develops in a marriage. When you don't answer their phone they get into many thoughts inside her brain, is he ok, why is he not picking up the phone, is he ignoring me, is he not able to hear the phone ring, ofcourse... the classic is he with someone else etc ? this is a natural thought process. With the technology at hand there are many ways you can help your wife alleviate from such frustrations, just send her a text message that you cannot answer or let her know ahead of time that you will not be able to take the call for whatever reason. Help her to not get frustrated when you forget things, ask her to send you a reminder message if something important is expected of you and you might not remember to do it.

Women are super multitaskers, or at least that's what we try and do. They tend to work on many things at the same time and can expect similar from you. It is ok if you are not able to make it?

Tips for Wife - Husband's way of thinking

Men like quiet time or me time more than women. They need their man cave or hangout with their friends. Get over it, be comfortable with it, in exchange, trade for your me-time and do things with your friends and family

Men are not used to expressing love or care directly. They show that they care by helping in a different perspective. Some are very expressive, however many men think that it is over exaggeration to express love to their spouse depending on the culture they come from. Understand it and respect it, tell them clearly what you want. It took me 5 years to make my husband understand that he need to give me some special gifts for my birthday at least balloons and flowers maybe :)

Don't complain about problems, Men do not like to hear about problems, they like to hear that you "need help". They will do anything to help. Tell them a problem and tell them what you think is a good solution and ask for their help and Bingo, your problem is solved. Be open to accept their way of helping and appreciate it genuinely

When they say something, it is literal, don't take the exaggerated meaning out of it.

Be straightforward when you need something too, ask them what you need, don't expect them to remember or figure out what you need. Tell them what you need exactly and let them do it for you.

When you need them to do something for you, ask for it in a polite way rather than asking as if your are ordering for it. Requests will go long way with your man as opposed to requirements or orders. If you persist on getting something, it may or may not happen based on how you are asking for it

Don't expect your husband to love you the same even after many fights, commit to your mistakes and ask for a sincere apology and commit to future behaviour if it is your mistake and try not to repeat that mistake like promised.

Make them feel very important in the relationship. Men like to be the man of the house and relationship. Giving them that place in the house is very important factor in relationship. No matter if your husband is a stay at home husband or if he earns a tons of money or runs a charity or you earn all the money, whatever is the case, make him feel special and let him be the man of the house. And you take pride in being a Women of the house, which is equally important.

Don't bother your husband much with childcare, unless he is really thriving for taking care, which is usually rare. Childcare is not their thing. There will be only few exceptions. It is absolutely normal for your husband not to show interest in changing daipers, feeding in the middle of the nights, feeding meals, shower, changing clothes whatever it is, doesn't matter how much they love their kids, they don't love the chores the babies comes with. Making them forcefully or guiltily taking care of the kids will only result in improper handling and resentment between the wife and the husband. It is just like asking you to do something you are not good at, no matter how much you try, you will not be able to deliver your best at such tasks. However this doesn't mean you are by yourself with child care, get help from parents, babysitters, older kids, other moms etc, and occasional help from your husband which can save your marriage a lifetime.

Give Love

Passion in Relationship

You can search throughout the entire universe for someone who is more deserving of your love and affection than you are yourself, and that person is not to be found anywhere. You yourself, as much as anybody in the entire universe deserve your love and affection.
---Buddha

The most important thing is to enjoy your life - to be happy - it's all that matters.
---Audrey Hepburn

When was the last time you celebrated a moment in your relationship. Life can quickly get caught up in current events and activities. Especially if you are working a fulltime job, have kids, have a business or other areas which take up your time and energy and by the time you come to relationship nurturing, it becomes the last priority.

Take a moment right now, and write down what are the three most important items you are expecting from your wife or husband? Is love or strong relationship on your list? If it is not on your list, then revisit and ensure it is on the list because, happy and strong relationship is the bottom-line for happiness in a relationship. To keep your relationship happy, there needs to be a sense of accomplishment and growth, and every time there is an accomplishment and growth made, you should celebrate it to keep enriching the relation.

Steps to build a long lasting passion in your relationship:
1. Be the influencer not the critic
2. Express love
3. Try new things together
4. Do a check point
5. Celebrate

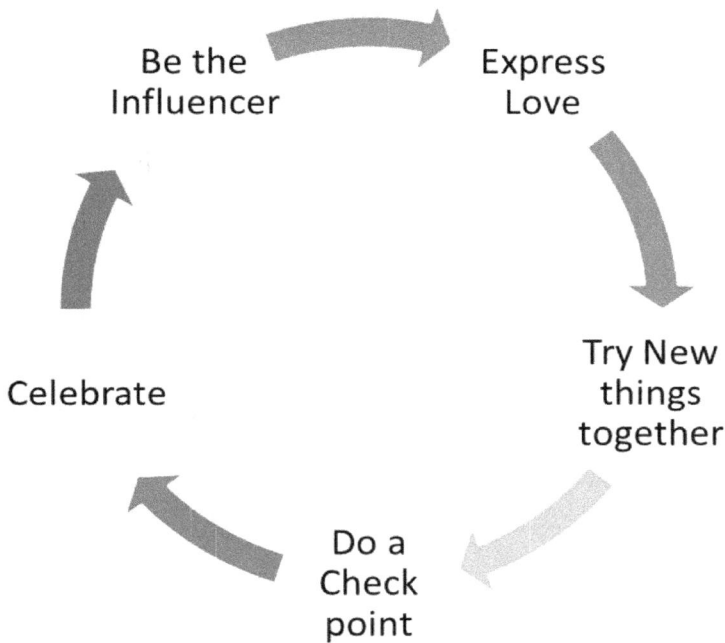

Be the influencer, not the critic:

Relationships mature due to the fact that couples understand each other well enough to get along for life time. Also, in every successful relationships one thing that is common is that the couples partner with each other and influence each other rather than critique one's shortcomings or weaknesses. Couples should practice the techniques to influence their spouse as opposed to disagreeing and causing conflicts that result in barriers in the relation.

We all want things to be done certain way, and there is a no way two people can do things in the same exact way. Doing things differently results in small to big clashes in a relationship. Couples can use this powerful tool to influence each other on the outcome rather than critic.

Express love:

Express love and gratitude often. Don't assume your spouse is aware of your love for them and that you appreciate all that they do for you. Instead say it, a simple thank you for the coffee, a morning kiss, a hug when back from work, a high five when something is accomplished goes a long way. Appreciation creates a positive vibe in one's mind and heart and increases the happiness levels. Send love messages to each other, a nice gift, some intimate time for each other, date nights all of these add up to loving relationship.

Try new things together:
Relationship can get routine when everyday is a routine and scheduled. Every once a while spice up things by trying new routine, or just trying a new thing together. It can be something as simple as sharing a new morning routine or trying out a new wine or checking out a new place, going on a hike, getting those bikes out and going out for a ride, starting a sport, or going to a gym together. Often when couples spend time as buddies, it brings out a different side of your spouse and will spark a new passion in the relationship.

Do a Checkpoint:
Unless you keep score, you will not know if you are moving forward or backward or at standstill. So, it is very important to take time once a month or more frequently and do a relationship assessment. This need not be a huge task, a simple self checking to ensure you are taking your relationship towards the right direction. These assessments will help you identify problems at the early stage which can be overcome with basic measures as opposed to finding issues too late.

Celebrate:

Celebration is key to happiness. Acknowledge, every small and big accomplishments and celebrate them with your spouse, your kids or family. Celebrations don't have to be expensive, it can be a simple glass of wine, or going out for an ice-cream, going on a long bike-ride, go on a hike, buying a small present, you get the point. Celebration brings the families together and creates a bonding of togetherness.

Secret to managing life successfully
~~~and to avoid falling into day to day PitFalls

How Wives changes After baby

For wife the news of having a baby changes her whole world, it is a very special feeling that she is now going to give birth to a baby and she gets to carry and nurture the baby in her body. This is one of the greatest things a woman can go through in her life. Or I can say this is the one greatest natural thing a woman can go through in her life. Usually women are less concerned about financial logistics of the baby and more concerned about the environment around them. Some couples might be staying in a studio apartment with more singles or unmarried couples around. Sometimes they might be living in a rental, sometimes they are probably living with in-laws and other family members, or they might be living in a neighborhood that is not very nice. What ever is the situation with living, women usually want to move to a new place where they can bring up with no concerns of safety, stress, smoke, adult life exposure and want to settle down in one place.

Women also go through many hormonal changes during pregnancy and are very emotionally sensitive during and little after the baby. They tend to exaggerate some issues and get way emotional on things than they should. This contributes a lot to not understanding what a husband is trying to do for the family. If husband comes home late from work trying to work overtime to make some extra money, the wife might get emotional and start crying that he doesn't love her anymore and likes to spend more time outside than with her and taking care of her. Small issues like these in the beginning will be ok, husband will make up for some and wife tries to keep her emotions in tight, but as some difficult times get added and when husband has no patience to deal with the emotional drama, it gets worse. Once again distance between wife and husband starts to grow and it only gets worse based on how many external factors are involved in the couple's life. When wife gets emotions and her parents or friends catch her in that moment they can give advice which will only turn worse in the relationship.

(Read my Go it Alone section for how to deal with relationship issues no matter what stage in life you are)

Second Baby Syndrome
Wife and Husband

Wife: Hey Honey, guess what I am not feeling very well since a last few days
Husband: Oh, did you eat something bad ?

Wife: No, I am feeling a little sick in the mornings
Husband: Oh my god, I hope its not what I am thinking
Wife: You are mean
Husband: What, I am not ready for a second baby
Wife: gets very sad in her heart.

Few days later
Wife: Honey, I did the home pregnancy test
Husband: OK and ?
Wife: happily says "It came positive, we are going to have a second baby"
Husband: I told you I am not ready for the second baby

Wife: Tears.....

This is a real life scenario. unfortunate isn't it? or are you saying so what if the husband is not ready for the second baby ?

Anyone who has had children especially the second or third baby went through this above scenario one or the other way where Husband has not stepped up or enjoyed the arrival news of the baby. And in all fairness many times it is the wife too that is not happy with the second or third baby, the point of the matter is there is always a different concern and less excitement when it comes to the second or third or fourth baby.

From Wife's point of view:

Many husbands change dramatically with the arrival of the second child on. Once the wife has a second baby, they don't see her as a loving partner anymore, they see wife as a child bearing machine and someone who is adding responsibilities to his plate. Instead of partnering with her and helping each other out, many husbands get into a its your problem, it's your task to change diapers, it's your task to take care of the baby in the nights etc. This is where wives feel lost, they often question why they are having a baby with a man who is not even ready to step up to the responsibility. Why doesn't he be like other men who still love their wife. With all these raging questions on mind, wife doesn't like to have sex with her husband anymore. With one kid it was probably not that bad for her to get back to her relationship quickly, however with the second baby, she's parenting a toddler or another kid and newborn during the day, nursing or feeding a baby all night, and also still has all the baby weight, there is no way she is feeling it. Not only is she feeling fat, but nursing eliminates sex drive hormonally, and her resentment toward her husband for whatever he's doing wrong with the toddler is not helping anything. She just feels he only loves her when he makes love to her and when it comes to responsibilities, he throws her under the bus. He just leaves her alone to deal with all the child related tasks and chores that drain her sanity, sleep and health. Women put on weight in many cases, they still have the baby fat, they overeat, they don't have time or energy to exercise, they feel sorry for them and indulge in fatty foods. Then they think they are not looking attractive anymore to make love to her spouse. So, between the rage and overweight and energy loss, they will end up not giving the husband what they still need after the baby, Love and sex. This creates further distance in the relationship, the distance that can quickly drag the man to infidelity or even divorce.

From Husband's point of view:

Second baby news is a mixed emotion for the dad. It doesn't bring any new happiness to him. It can instead bring more worries and anxiety that there will be additional responsibilities and more work and his wife for whom he was the #1 will now become even lower priority. Men needs to feel that importance in a relationship in order for them to stay engaged in it. With the introduction of second child that importance fades away from the wife's perspective.

Suddenly the wife is all about the kids, there are no personal conversations with the husband about what is his favorite movie, "should I cook you your favorite food today?", can we watch a movie together….. nothing that was once an exciting thing to do is no more fun for the wife. At this time husband starts thinking his wife is boring and an irritable person. She gets mad more often, doesn't clean his clothes, doesn't sleep in the same room, doesn't make love to him and is always worried about the kids and all that is around them as if she is the only one loving them. Problems start to build up, stress from work and household chores, never ending child care and even as they grow after school activities, their projects, baseball, soccer game create more and more distance, exhaustion, and resentment. This is a tipping point in many couples marriage. Many couples go down the path of divorce thinking they married the wrong person and that they are not compatible. Only if they knew that they are not the only ones going through this and if they can play smart in the relationship, things would be different.

In the section Leverage Help, I discuss some very basic ways to combat the energy and sanity drain that moms go through after having a child especially the second or third.

Impactful Tips for couples struggling

1. Be courteous to each other, it's not about who is more tired, it's not about who is changing more diapers, it's not about who is not sleeping through the night. It is about being caring to each other and

understand that it is equally difficult for each other to make past the phase

2. Put a schedule and take turns to take care of kids, respect the schedule and appreciate and do something caring to your spouse to show the appreciation. Positive reinforcement goes long way and creates a positive vibe in the environment

3. Give each other a break completely from kids for at least 1 full day in a two-week period, if possible ask grandma, grandpa, babysitter to come and take care of the kids while you take a break.

4. Don't make abrupt decisions when things are not going well. It is important that you remember that our emotions are like roller coaster ride especially when we are going through hormonal changes and stress and sleep deprivation. Just give it a day or two and give time to clear the air.

5. Start having your romance again, even if you're not feeling it. Really, just do it.

6. Show appreciation to your spouse for even small things. Let him/her or her feel extra special by showing appreciation and gratitude

7. If husband is disconnected and doesn't want to help with the kids, IT IS OK, I am not joking, IT IS OK and normal for the husband not willing to help, just move on, give him the space and leverage his help for other areas and get help from other sources for your childcare.

8. It is ok if your body is not back in shape, remember motherhood is blessing, enjoy your baby fat and do some nice things, dress yourself pretty, go out to play, have girls night, get involved with a community event, there are many things you can do that has nothing to do with if you are back in shape or not.

9. Start a new hobby, and look-into helping others or shift your focus to a new passion to keep you motivated on the days you are feeling low.

10. Try out date nights, if you cannot afford a babysitter and cannot do a complete night out, try to do night at home, make the kids sleep and enjoy a glass of wine together or watch a movie while eating dinner to bring back the connectedness.

11. Don't criticize each other or parents, there is a high possibility you will be surrounded with many people and endless tasks to accomplish, try to be nice to each other and avoid small talk and gossips as much possible.

12. Eat healthy and get moving, no matter how busy your schedule gets, try and squeeze in healthy meals, green juice for breakfast will give you a good start.

13.   Get out of the house, don't stay all day inside the house. It's good for the kids and for you too to get some fresh air and break the day to day pattern of routine. Keep an hour or two everyday to do something that involves outside the house.

14.   Take a vacation or break from work, no matter how busy your work is and how less money you have to spend for vacation, just plan and take a vacation from work and day to day stress.

15.   Be part of a community or friends club or fitness club. It is important to surround yourself with friends and or family that you can escape to every once a while. Now there should be a balance on how much you will escape to keep your relationship healthy.

Leverage Help

First things first, acceptance is key to success. Accept that your life has changed after marriage and even more after kids, and work together as a team to come up with some practical compromises and ways to make your lives better. Accept that it is ok if things are not perfect, if the house gets messy, laundry gets piled up. The sooner you realize it is ok not to have control on everything and it is ok to not be perfect all the times the better it is for you.

Get some help!! There is help everywhere, if you need and ask for it. Some could be paid help and some could be an exchange help. If you can afford go for a babysitter on a daily basis or even a live in nanny. They can take care of the baby and cook and clean the house, it is well worth the money spent. Or hire a helper on hourly basis, or find a home daycare where they can take care of your baby for a lower price. Or do a exchange help, you let your spouse help with the kids, (remember to not criticize one another's parenting) so you get a break, or take care of a friends kids one day and send your kids to theirs another. Sometimes older siblings can be more help than a real babysitter, it is completely OK to take help from your older daughter or son. What I strongly believe in is that you spend quality time and teach great principles to your older or first child and he or she will take the torch forward with the rest of your kids along with you. Sometimes, second or third one will step up faster on the principles and rules than the first one, and that is ok too.

There are many creative options to get help, you can hire a housekeeper twice a month or based on your schedule, get your groceries delivered, home therapy, designated alone time for socializing/working out for each parent. This is a good time to also leverage family and extended family, see if someone in your family like parents or grandparents can help. Most of the times they won't mind, instead they would love to. In fact parents are a good source of help both physically and emotionally during tough times. Sometime help could come in the form of neighbor's teenage kids. They can help with many things too, from helping with baby chores to helping tutoring older kids to helping with housekeeping. The point I want to make is that help will be available if you look for and I strongly recommend to get help in one or the other way rather than doing it alone. There are many other things that you can purpose your time when you are freed with some of the mundane tasks that you can get help.

Phases in life as a couple

Phase I: Getting started – life is beautiful

You found your life partner or maybe your parents found you one and you are now engaged will be getting married soon. In the beginning of a relationship, everything seems to be wonderful, everyone is at best behavior and trying to impress. There is not much confusion here as the couple don't usually face any life crisis, solve any financial issues, or are deal with any major responsibility. This is more of a just getting started phase. There will be minor issues if anything. The relationship is young and so is the couple, there is immaturity and not too much ego. Quick fights and very quick patches is what it takes this phase most of the time. By the end of this phase you are married and living together.

Phase II: settling – reality kicks in

You are married and now starting a new life, you are trying to find a place for you and your spouse to live. There is lots of love and affection at this time, and you compromise for each other's tastes and pick and choose furniture, dishes, home decor, electronics, jewelry, clothes etc. Late night movie time, dinner, pubs, friends, family most of the time is spent getting to know the real each other, each other's parents and each other's real likes and dislikes. There are many things that you don't expose to each other that come to the light after marriage while settling in. There will be areas of interest that you thought you had a good idea what your husband or wife liked and after marriage it is all of a sudden turning out to be a new experience everyday. This is when reality strikes into the relationship. Most of the times the focus is diverted back to settling into the relationship. Most of the time in this phase is spent fighting, sadness, patchup, catch up, sorries, vacations, trips. This phase is basically a roller coaster ride of Fun, Happiness, Fights, Makeup, little bit of Did I marry the right person, Fun, Happiness, I love you.

Phase III: first kid - compromises

By the time the couples start to get into too many further conflicts, they hear the news of the arrival of a baby, which changes the dynamics of the relationship all over. The couples feel more connected and bonded together during this special times in their lives. First baby brings that missing happiness in a couple who are wondering why they married each other, if they married the right person, how they can fix the relationship and so on.

With the arrival of the first baby, most of these thoughts go into a back burner, "I never really loved my husband, but I love my kids and that is enough for us to stay together" one of my friends said who was struggling with her relationship. "I would like to move on, but when I look at my kids and how much my wife loves and cares for our baby, makes me just forget every pain we had in our relation and brings me back to my wife" another friend says.

Phase IV: expansion – spouse is an alien
Once more kids come into life, family is now more into routine, bringing up the kids, saving money to buy a own house to give a better living to the family, and one or the other way couples get themselves tied into never ending debts. Which will make them weak financially.

Many spend way too much money than what they can afford. Then the relationship starts to strain again. There is no more money for date nights, or hiring a sitter and getting personal time. Some don't even want to spend money to go see their parents, cousins or family and friends. Intimacy is least on priorities. Working late at work, fights for who does what chores over and over. Spouses developing new habits and finding new friendships. Like two strangers living together under one roof.

Phase VI: Done for this Life – or maybe not

Kids are grown up and less responsibilities with respect to taking care of them and less financial stress. Chances are one of the partners of parents of the partners have a health issue by now, senior care kicks in, appreciation of parents, and feeling of gratitude seeing the parents in the vulnerable state changes the anger and frustrations on the spouse. Couples get used to each other by now and spend time with each other on the things they never got to do.

Don't wait to enjoy life after something is accomplished, enjoy every moment and the journey of life.

Life is too short, everyone is going to be gone one day, it is not important to fight over petty issues which mean nothing in overall grand scheme of things. Don't lose sight of the beautiful Journey you are here for on earth and make use of it to the fullest.

My mantra:
Live Life to the Fullest and Have Fun